Printed in the United States of America

ISBN 978-1535222914

Published by

Law Offices of Allen M. Leung
4482 Barranca Parkway, Suite 118
Irvine, CA 92604

Table of Contents

About the Authors

Allen M. Leung & Winnie H. Shiao,
Attorneys-at-Law
Husband And Wife

As attorneys, Mr. Leung and Ms. Shiao have a long and distinguished record of helping our community. From college admissions to financial aid, we've stuck to our mission of disseminating information to help those in need.

Specifically, we are authors of "Education Judo: How Asians Can Win the College & Financial Aid Game" and "Writing Like a Lawyer: EZ-to-Learn Templates and Formulas." Those books were written as part of our proposed solution to issues we've tackled in the past, namely College Admissions and Financial Aid, as well as "writing templates" for those who don't like to write.

For more information on them, please read through the "Introduction" section.

ACKNOWLEDGEMENTS

We want to acknowledge our valuable members of our office staff for their research, review and edit of this Book.

A Huge THANK YOU to the following: Monica Lee, Michael Ko, Chris Wang, and Vicki Fan.

And of course, our eternal debt of gratitude to Mr. Che-Hsun (Thomas) Wan, our modern day “Zhuge Liang” grandmaster strategist, who tirelessly thought of all our marketing slogans and plans, and who encouraged us to “connect all the different dots” of our passions and business for spiritual and personal growth.

Finally, we also like to acknowledge our roots and show deference to some historical figures far in the past, to a time that’s known as the “Age of Three Kingdoms” in China. During that time, many historical commenters observed that if the famous general Cao Cao (known for his decisiveness) and Zhuge Liang (known for his strategic battle plans) were on the same side of a battle, the chance for victory would drastically increase.

With this Book, we are providing a decisive “Strategic Plan” to increase ***Your*** chance of victory to protect your assets as well as to reduce your taxes, and perhaps to leave a lasting legacy lasting for generations.

We could not have completed this book without everyone’s help and encouragement. Thank you!

Disclaimer

All of the scenarios presented herein are hypothetical and for illustrative purposes only. Nothing herein shall be deemed or construed as providing legal advice. Such scenarios presented in this book have some basic assumptions which may not be applicable to individual readers of this book.

Since everyone's situation is different, we urge each reader to consult his or her tax attorney or tax CPA for specific questions regarding YOUR background and specifications, and YOUR needs.

Introduction

As lawyers, our goal is to help the community, especially those issues affecting our Asian/Chinese community. A few years ago, we saw that Asian-American students were having trouble gaining admission to top 25 colleges.

Furthermore, parents were facing a tough dilemma of paying for their kids' increasing education costs versus saving for their retirement. We asked ourselves: Is there a way to help kids pay for their education WITHOUT compromising parents' retirement account?

The answer was an emphatic YES! We discovered a way to obtain the maximum amount of financial aid (cash – grants and scholarships and not loans) from colleges. And what colleges provide the most generous financial aid? The highest **ranking private colleges**.

Since gaining admission to the highest private colleges posed an immense challenge due to their low admission rates, we began to help students overcome obstacles and gain admission. Indeed, our statement "Top Colleges and Financial Aid" is not just a simple advertising slogan; ***it's actually our missions for our community.***

Our College Admission Results

Over the past 4 years culminating with the high school graduating class of 2016, we have helped the following students gain admission into: Harvard (12), Yale (10), Stanford (5), Princeton (7), Brown (6), Columbia (6), Cornell (19), Dartmouth (11), Penn (6), UChicago (3), MIT (5), Cal Tech (6), Northwestern (11), Johns Hopkins (11), USC (60), Williams (19), Amherst (12), UC-Berkeley (99), UCLA (83), UC San Diego (129), and ***Many Others*** Top Colleges.

Our Financial Aid Results

Equally as impressive is our record for Financial Aid (grants and scholarships, NOT loans). For the past 3 years alone (again ending with High School Class of 2016, we've obtain a total of **$100 Million** (4 year rate for attending college) for our parents and students. For the Class of 2016 alone, we've obtain a four year rate of $45 Million.

To break it down to a per family basis: we are able to obtain an average of ***$50,000 per year*** in financial aid for private colleges and ***$20,000 per year*** for UC colleges.

We are confident our results exceed many of those so-call "academies" or "institutes" on the market. Add in the amount of financial help received by our parents and students, we are proud to say that **no one comes close to our record.**

So How Does College Admissions & Education Have to do With Asset Protection and Tax Savings?

In a word – **Everything!**

After we've helped families gain admission to top colleges and obtain financial aid, we recognized middle-aged parents faced yet ANOTHER problem: retirement.

With our strong record of solving problems, parents again asked us to advise them on ways to save on taxes and preserve their hard-earned money and assets. It's such demand in the marketplace that has led us to writing this Book.

Looking around the marketplace, there are no books that focus on asset protection and tax minimization in an "easy to understand" format. So we decided to tackle this issue -- again based on our knowledge of tax law. Believing that knowledge is power, we set out to solve another big problem.

When we decide to tackle this important issue, we will once again utilize our knowledge of law. Readers can expect that we are going to make a lasting impact and present a viable solution for those who need it.

If we could obtain $100 Million in college financial aid, we can confidently say that our goal is to save **our Clients $1 Billion** in current and future taxes.

Our Proposal to Solve This Problem

Through Education. That's right -- through sharing our knowledge. We believe by sharing our knowledge through seminars and this book, people of all ages can learn ways to legally save taxes and protect their assets. Another big concern of middle age parents is asset protection and legacy. This book address all these issues. As lawyers, we always wish to bring information to those in need.

Sharing the Knowledge

Just like the way we solved the "Education Problem," we will turn to our knowledge of the law – and spread such knowledge to those who want to learn. In the age of Internet, we strongly believe in information sharing so we can get the "conversation going." Thus, Education is key to solving this pressing issue, as knowledge is power.

What Will This Book Teach Me?

There are many books and information on the Internet with titles such as "How to Retire Comfortably" or "How to Make Money in Real Estate." However, many of such books skip over the tax savings aspect. We will provide concrete examples so readers can understand easily. Specifically, we wish to focus on the following areas.

Asset Protection

Many readers of this Book are probably middle-aged parents who wish to protect and preserve their assets after many years of hard work. What could be "enemies" of one's assets? Well, lawsuits and taxes are the most common foes of one's hard-earned money. We will provide you "tools" to defend against such adversaries, including knowledge of tax laws, trusts, and setting up companies.

There are many books and information on the Internet about setting up companies to shield personal liability. Thus, we will not go into that too much in our Book. Rather, we will delve into subject matters that others don't discuss as much.

No matter what you do, the primary focus of any strategy should be to decrease your taxes. And there are actually laws in place already that help you achieve this goal.

Estate Planning

Regarding the issue of legacy, we have also included a chapter on "Estate Planning." Normally a "dry" subject, we utilize illustrations to bring some "spice" to this subject area. Simply put, Estate Planning goes "hand-in-hand" with Asset Protection and Tax Minimization.

For Estate Planning, we will introduce Living Trusts, a Must-Have in Estate Planning. We will cover two types of Living Trust: revocable and irrevocable and show you how they can be used so your kids pay NO Estate Tax. Even better, we will show readers that there is an easy way to avoid amending one's trust even when one buys a new house, opens a new bank account, etc.

Perhaps many readers have heard of Living Trusts and thinking that it only consists of one document. We actually prefer to refer to it as a "Living Trust Package," as it includes Wills, Durable Powers of Attorneys, Nomination of Guardian for minor children, and Advanced Healthcare Directive.

Legacy

Many immigrant families, whether old or new, still cling to an old belief that "family fortune can't pass for more than three generations." Again, we have solutions for that ***dilemma***, and they are outlined in this Book. To give readers a preview, it involves setting up a special type of trust that **guarantees** avoidance of paying any amount of estate tax. In fact, this family asset protection strategy is used by many of American's rich and famous families, including Rockefellers, Kennedys, etc. AND now we are revealing this to "ordinary people," so they can take advantage of this type of Trust law.

How Will the Book Teach Me?

How? Through **concepts and illustrations!** That's right: instead of long and wordy explanations, we will use easy-to-understand illustrations to understand key concepts. AND instead of presenting to readers many tax laws that have NO effects on personal finance, we ONLY focus those tax laws most important to personal finance and small investors. So in other words, we've already done the hard part, and we are presenting to the readers in an "easy-to-understand" format – that could even make learning about tax law ***FUN***.

Thus, this book will teach readers, from middle age parents to high-school or college age young adults, concepts they need to protect their assets and minimize taxes. We also suggest that they pass this knowledge to their friends, because if one learns these concepts when young, their assets can grow and appreciate, even if the rate of return is conservative. Even for middle-age parents, it's NOT too late to learn these concepts. Since they most likely have MORE assets now than before, they MUST learn "Asset Protection" concepts, through taxation law, to preserve those assets and pass to the ***next generation TAX-FREE*** and/or establish their lasting legacy.

~ Allen Leung and Winnie H. Shiao

CHAPTER ONE: Four Tax Laws One Must Know

There are many sections of tax laws out there and based on our knowledge, we have distilled all the different sections of tax laws into the following four that everyone who's interested in Asset Protection and reduction of Taxes Must Know.

Again, this is what Taxpayer, from young to old, must know in various stages of their lives to save BIG on taxes. Just applying the knowledge in these laws, you will save much more of your hard earned money and perhaps use the money saved to create a lasting legacy.

So let's get to it!

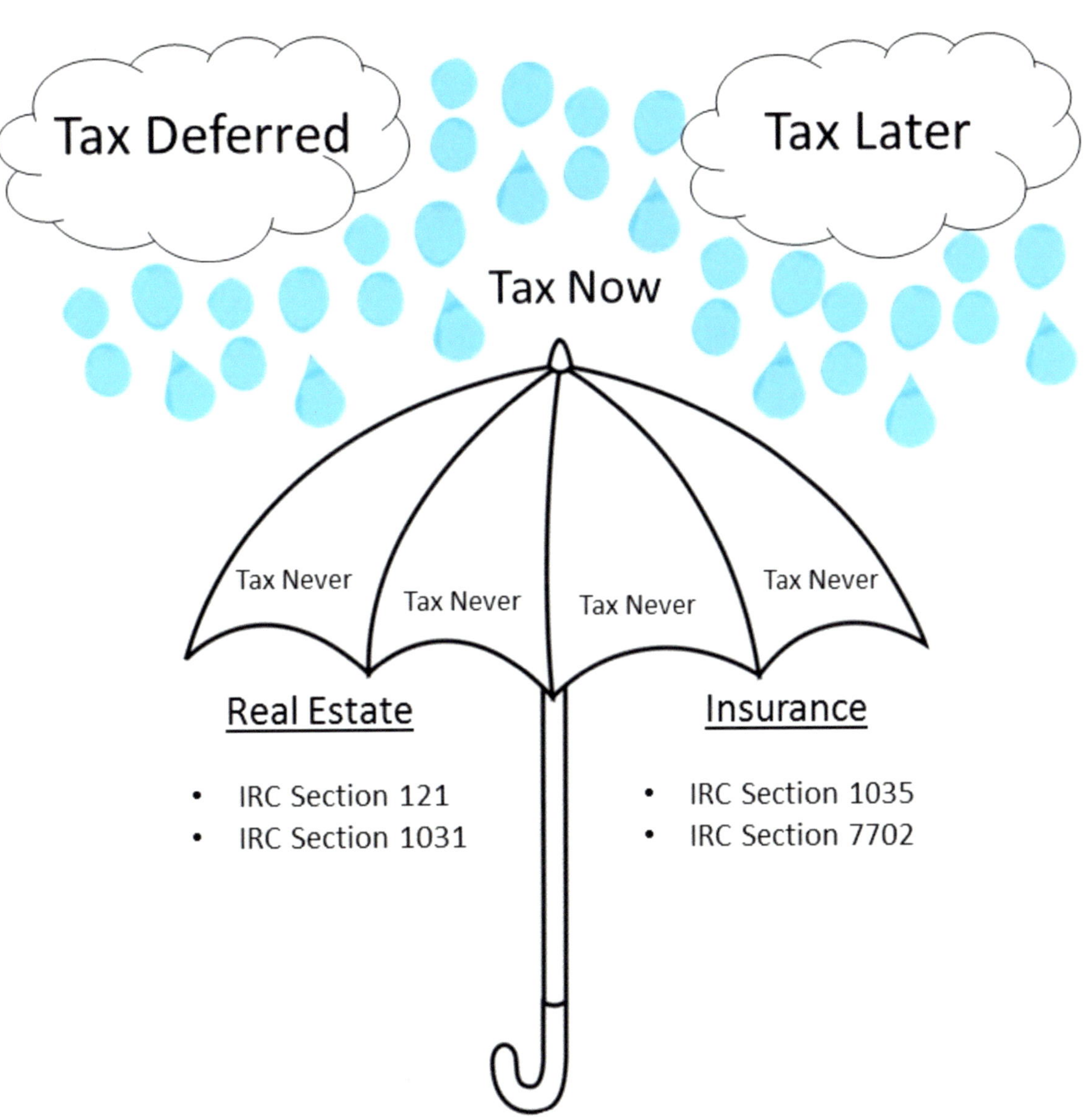
Tax Deferred
Tax Later
Tax Now
Tax Never
Tax Never
Tax Never
Tax Never
Real Estate
• IRC Section 121
• IRC Section 1031
Insurance
• IRC Section 1035
• IRC Section 7702

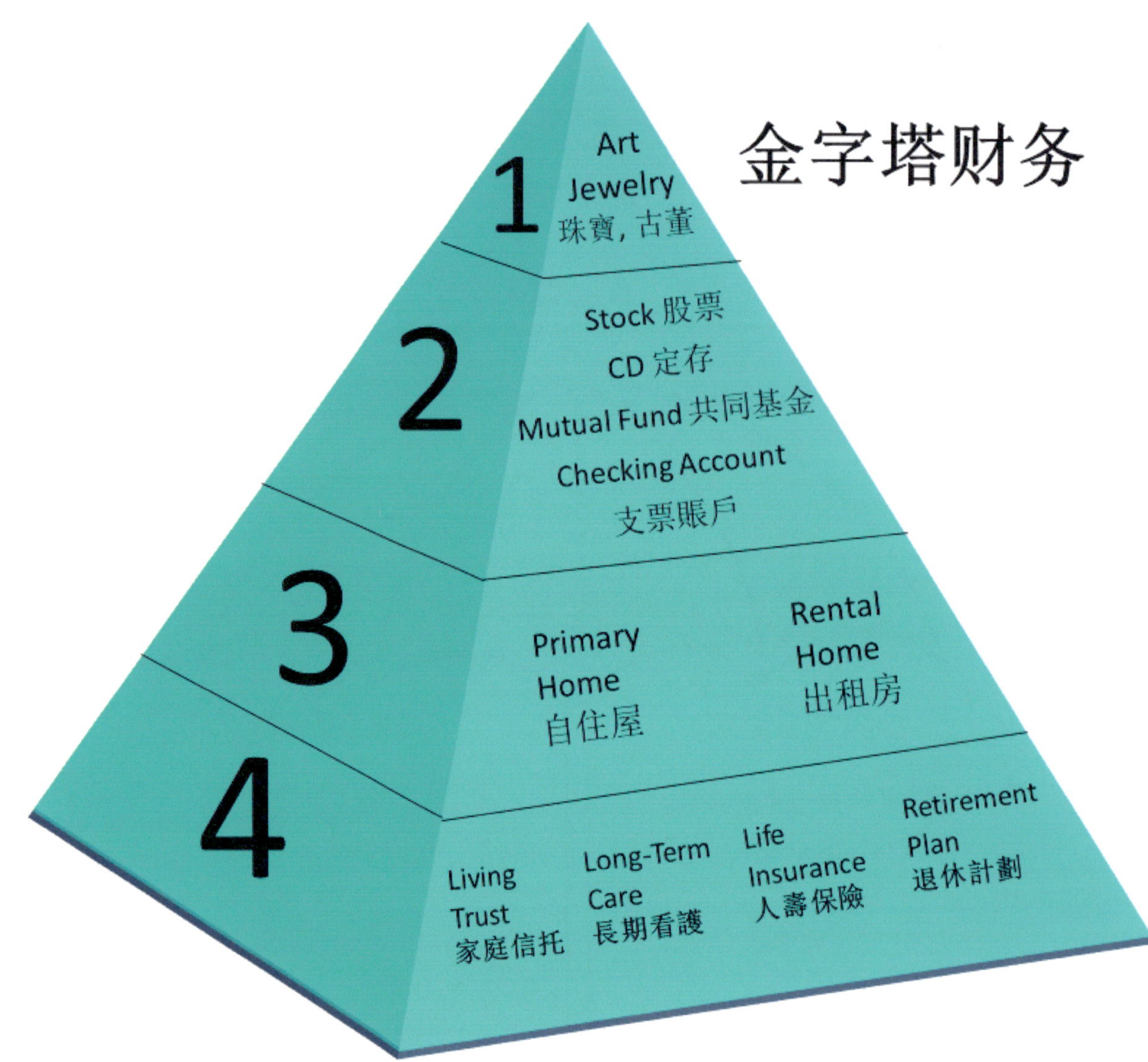
金字塔财务
1
Art
Jewelry
珠寶, 古董
2
Stock 股票
CD 定存
Mutual Fund 共同基金
Checking Account
支票賬戶
3
Primary
Home
自住屋
Rental
Home
出租房
4
Living
Trust
家庭信托
Long-Term
Care
長期看護
Life
Insurance
人壽保險
Retirement
Plan
退休計劃

(A) IRC Section 121

Under this section, a married couple can claim exemption up to $500,000 of capital gains for sale of their "primary residence" home ($250,000 gain exemption for a single person).

Even better: you don't actually have to live in the house when you sell. Section 121 allows $500,000 exemption as long as the homeowners lived there "2 out of past 5 years, and such days of "living there" do not need to be consecutive.

<u>Example</u>: If a couple has bought a house on 6/1/11 for $500,000 and decide to sell it on 6/1/16 for $1,000,000, having lived there all the time. Then the house has a capital gain of $500,000. If the couple decides to sell the house, normally they would have to pay about 25 percent of the gain in taxes (15 percent federal and 10 percent CA tax). Under 121 Tax Code, **they could save themselves about $125K** (25% x $$500K gain) worth of capital gain!

The KEY here is NOT that they lived in the home for 5 years; rather, it's that lived in their home for MORE THAN 2 years.

Example: Husband and Wife lives in buys and moves in a "House A" on 1/1/2012. **The purchase price = $500,000.** They lived in "House A" as primary residence for 2.5 years and then moved into "House B" (which they purchased on 7/1/2014. After ***renting*** out "House A" (becomes investment home) <u>for two years</u>, they now want to sell *House A*. After only 2 weeks on the market, they received an offer for *House A* at <u>$950,000</u>, which they accepted. **House A** is due to close escrow on October 1, 2016.

Question: <u>How Much Tax on the Capital Gains</u>, if ANY, do Husband and Wife need to pay on Sale of "House A" – assuming the deal closes escrow on September 1, 2016?

The following is the way to analyze Sec 121. First, you look at the "close of escrow" sale date. Here, it's 9/1/16. You then **go back 5 years – to 9/1/11.**

Then ask a simple question: did you live there for 2 years (2 x 365 days = 730 days in total)? Again, the days of living in "primary home" ***does NOT need*** to be consecutive.

Tax Savings

So the Answer is $0 if you KNOW the law.

If you do NOT know the law, you will be paying TWO types of taxes: federal (15% on capital gains) and CA State tax (approx. 10%). The capital gain in this case is $450,000 ($950,000 sales price – $500,000 purchase price).

25% (15% federal + 10% state) x $450,000 = **$112,500 in Tax!!**

Putting the value of money to work, $112,500 in year 2016 **will be worth $305,000** (almost tripling) ***in 30 years***, assuming a 3.5% rate of inflation.

So WHY there is NO tax in this case if you know the Law? Please read the part on Section 121 (of Internal Revenue Code) inside this Book.

121 國家稅務法

- 個人擁有房屋兩年
- 在過去的5年中在該房屋
- 積累居住2年
- 可以享受個人25萬/夫婦50萬的資本利得免稅

(B) IRC Section 1031

While Section 121 focused on "Primary Home," Section 1031 focused on "investment real estate." Basically, Section 1031 allows for "tax-free exchange" if one sells Investment Property A and exchanged for Property B (whose value is greater or equal to Property A).

The owner has 45 days to identify a MAXIMUM of three replacement properties within 45 calendar days after the property has been relinquished. The proprietor has a maximum of 180 days after the property has been relinquished to complete the 1031 exchange.

1031 Exchange can only qualify for real property. What are NOT included in the 1031 exchange are examples of: 1) Stock or Property HELD FOR SALE, 2) Stocks, Bonds or Notes, 3) Securities of evidence of indebtedness or interest, 4) Interests in partnership, 5) Beneficial Interests.

1031 Exchange could only be used regarding transaction on "real property." Items may include real estate, businesses, vehicles, objects of ownership, and "like-kind" property.
b. In order for a 1031 exchange to qualify, the property you purchase must be like-kind to the property you are going to buy.

Sellers CANNOT touch their property in between the sale of their old property and the purchase of their new property. By law the taxpayer must use an independent third party, usually an Escrow company, to handle the change. The function of the exchange partner/intermediary is to prepare the documents required by the IRS at the time of the sale of the old property and at the time of the purchase of the new property.

Example: You purchase Property A for $550,000 and sold Property A for $1,200,000 and you wish to purchase a property B for $1,200,000.

Question: How to make this deal without paying taxes?

Answer: By using 1031 Exchange. You can "trade up" from $550K property to $1.2 Million ***tax-free***.

How: You leave the proceeds of sale of Property A in Escrow and use that to purchase Property B. The sale of Property A and Property B **must NOT be more than 180 days apart.** One last requirement, you would need to identify Property B within 45 days of selling Property A.

Thus, Section 1031 gain exemption could be ***MORE THAN $500K***.

Example:

If you sell your property for $550,00 and you wish to purchase a property for $400,000, then you can use the 1031 Exchange and take your sold property's $400,000 into the new property without any taxes. HOWEVER the REMAINING DIFFERENCE between the two properties, which in this case, is <u>$150,000 will be TAXED</u>.

Question: Can one theoretically keep on doing 1031 Exchange (i.e. keep on "flipping" properties) without paying capital gains tax **for life**?

Answer: YES! One could exchange from a small condo all the way to a shopping plaza, and NEVER have to pay for capital gain tax, by engaging in 1031 Exchange correctly. Basically, when your heirs inherit the property, the original tax basis is "stepped up" to the market value, and thus NO capital gains tax when your heirs sell the property at that time.

1031交換

1031 交換 → 房地產最有效的延稅方法 (like-kind 同類交換)

1031 交換 → 國家稅務法第一款第一項 (1921年為了刺激國內經濟而制定的條例)

Rental Home
出租房

2006 購買 $200,000
Depreciation 折舊多年 (已折舊$100,000)
Adjusted tax basis 調整後的稅基 $100,000

2016 賣價$500,000

方案一:

2006 年

Tax Basis (成本價)	$200,000
— Depreciation (折舊)	$100,000
Adjusted tax basis (調整後的成本)	**$100,000**

2016 年

賣價$500,000

資本利得(capital gain) $400,000

A) 15% x 30 萬 (純收入50萬-20萬）
=$45,000

B) 25% x 10 萬折舊
=$25,000

聯邦稅 A + B = **$65,000**

必須繳交$65,000的稅

方案二:

(利用1031交換的延稅條款)

價值對等 Or 以小換大
→ 毋需付聯邦稅65,000
→ 延稅擴大投資效果

聯邦稅: A) 15% 資本利得
B) 25% 折舊回加
加州稅: 7 %
} 1031 可延稅

1031 可交換的物業種類
一家庭、二家庭、四家庭公寓、渡假屋、土地、辦公樓、旅館購物中心

不可用1031交換的種類
合夥人股份, 股票共同基金庫存, 個人主要自住屋

1031交換

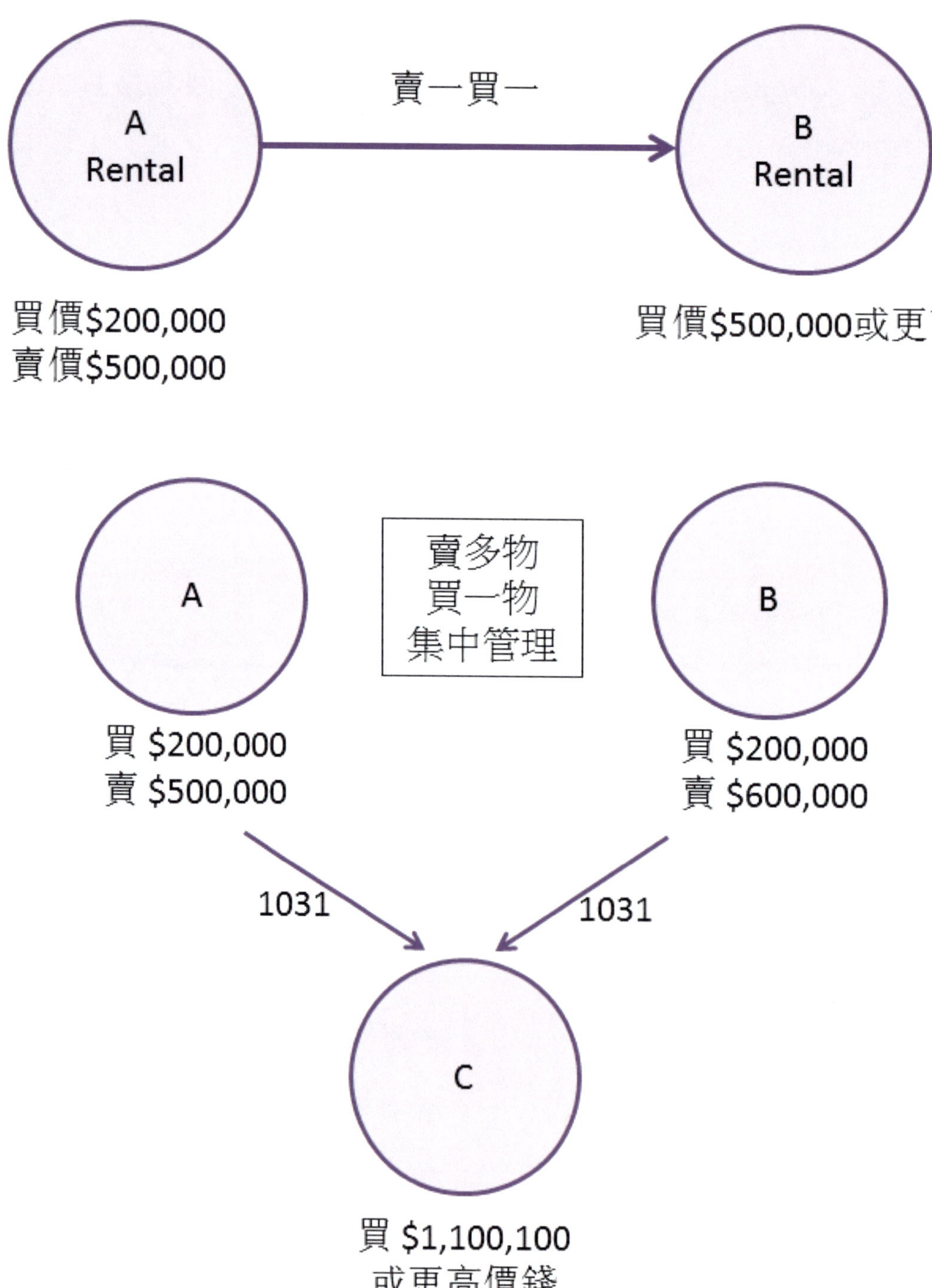

A
Rental
賣一買一
B
Rental
買價$200,000
賣價$500,000
買價$500,000或更高
A
賣多物
買一物
集中管理
B
買 $200,000
賣 $500,000
買 $200,000
賣 $600,000
1031
1031
C
買 $1,100,100
或更高價錢

1031交換

賣一買多
一物業→變多物業
豐富投資內涵

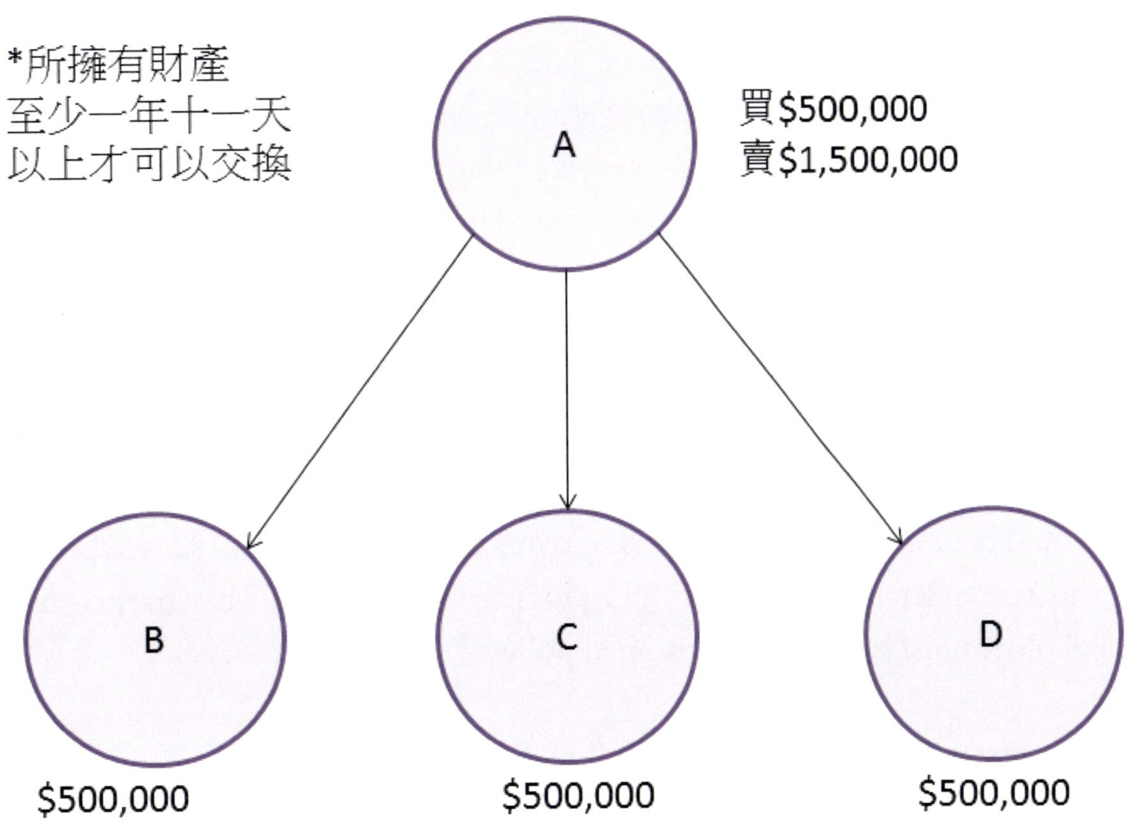

(C) IRC Section 1035

While Section 1031 dealt with investment "real property, Section 1035 deals with tax-free exchange of certain "paper assets" – life insurance and annuities. However, the exchange must be "like-kind" – i.e. must be between annuity contract OR between life insurance contracts; it CANNOT be between an Annuity contract and a Life Insurance one, or vice versa.

1. Basically, if you want to exchange your current life insurance, endowment or annuity policy to a new policy, then there will be no tax on the gain in the original policy at the time of the exchange, provided that there are no outstanding loans on the original policy. If you DO NOT do a 1035 exchange, then the gain from the original life insurance will be taxed as ordinary income.

2. Even if there are no gains in the life insurance policy, it is in the best interest of the owner to complete a 1035 exchange from one policy to another in order to AVOID a modified endowment contract (MEC). If the policyholder creates a MEC, that would take the Owner **outside the protection of Section 7702**, and he would have to surrender the old policy and purchase a new one. That means that the policyholder must surrender the original policy's cash value!

3. The purpose of Section 1035 is to allow flexibility to owners of Annuity or Life Insurance policies. Just like Section 1031, if you don't like a certain investment property you own, you should be able to exchange for another one *tax-free*. Perhaps you wish to move up from a single-family investment property to a **multi-tenant** in vestment property.

Section 1035 is the same way. Specifically, the owner may wish to increase coverage of from another policy while paying an equal or ***even lower amount of premium***. If Section 1035 does not exists, consumer would be "stuck" with the old policy. Thus, just like Sections 121 and 1031, Section 1035 aims to protect consumers, by allowing them a ***tax-free choice***.

(D) IRC Section 7702

As one of the more versatile sections of tax law, Section 7702 combines some of the very best attributes of retirement plans (IRA's and 401k). Basically, Section 7702 allows holders of certain contracts to enjoy tax-deferred growth. BUT unlike IRA's or 401k's, when one withdraws money from Section 7702 accounts, there is way to do so in a TAX-FREE way.

The easiest way to understand Section 7702 is to first review the popular retirement plan "vehicles" – IRA, Roth IRA and 401k plans.

Common Retirement Plans

Currently, IRA, Roth IRA and 401k plans all have some limitations. For the year 2016, the maximum Roth IRA & Traditional IRA contribution is $5,500 ($6.500 if age 50 or above). But Roth IRA has income limitation (maximum income of $194,000 for married couples. For Traditional IRA

As for traditional IRA, the income limit for marries couples is even LOWER, at $118,000 for year 2016.

For those whose employer offer 401k Plans, one could contribute the maximum amount of $18,000 per person for Year 2016.

While traditional IRA and 401(k) plans are tax-deferred, any withdrawal would be taxed at ordinary income tax rate starting when owner reaches 59.5 years old.

All of these popular retirement plans offer tax-free growth on gains of your investments inside such accounts. But what about those people who couldn't qualify based on income or whose employers don't offer 401k plans? Are they out of luck?

And wouldn't it be great NOT to have contribution limits AND to experience tax-free or tax-deferred growth for a large amount (or even **Unlimited**) of investment? If there is such a retirement plan, surely many people would be interested to at ***least inquire further***.

That's where Section 7702 comes in. In addition all the positive tax-deferral attributes, there is potential NO limit on how much a person could contribute,

AND there's an easy way to withdraw money tax-free (**unlike** Traditional IRA and 401k plans). Thus, if one understands these popular retirement plans, then Section 7702 is very easy to understand.

There is just one further requirement of Section 7702 – it must be part of a life insurance contract, offering the owner possibly even more protection.

Does Section 7702 applies to all life insurance policies? Not exactly, it only applies to those life insurance contracts which allows Owners thereof to possess cash-value. Thus, Section 7702 does NOT extend to "term life" insurance, which does not has any cash value.

Inheritance

Then what about inheritance to one's heirs? Is there any difference versus those common retirement plans? Mostly, tax consequences are the same; i.e. your beneficiaries would receive the investment value of those accounts ***income tax-free***. (There could be estate tax consequences, depending on the size of one's estate and the estate tax exemption for the year of which the owner passed away).

How Section 7702 Could Help You

Any law section that allows tax-deferral, perhaps permanent, deserves a closed look. The fact that Section 7702 does not limit income contribution means that, given enough time and based on concept of compound return, such investment could grow into a value many times of the original investment. Again, if the estate tax exemption is large enough for the year that owner passed away, the heirs would receive everything, plus additional death benefits **ALL tax-free**.

Thus, readers are advised to contact licensed professional, attorneys, CPA, personal finance advisors and insurance licensees to design a customized plan catering to his or her needs to take advantage of the tax benefits of Section 7702.

Finally, Section 7702 is the law section that many of America's richest families used to pass their wealth down – generation after generation. With Section 7702 and proper planning, a family could do the same and pass on their hard-earned assets to future generations tax-free and create a legacy lasting forever.

CHAPTER TWO: Basic Living Trusts (Revocable)

Living Trusts

A living trust is a legal document that establishes a trust to place your assets that will be transferred to your designated beneficiaries upon your death.

Why Establish a Living Trust?

1. **Avoids Probate** – Under California law, any estate with a gross value over $150,000 is subject to probate. Probate means that a court decides the distribution of the estate. By having a living trust, you can avoid probate by assigning designated beneficiaries who will receive your assets.

2. **Protect Assets** – Without a living trust, there is no guarantee that your designated beneficiaries will receive the assets in your estate. The court can distribute your estate in a manner that may not be in your desired interest. A living trust will ensure that your designated beneficiaries will receive the assets in the estate without interference from the court.

3. **Saves Money** – When your estate goes into probate, your designated beneficiaries will need to hire attorneys to represent them in court. The cost of probate attorneys is far higher than setting up a living trust. By setting up a living trust, you will not incur the high cost of probate attorneys.

4. **Saves Time** – When your estate is in probate, your designated beneficiaries will not have access to the assets in your estate. By setting up a living trust, your designated beneficiaries will have access to the assets in your estate upon your death.

5. **Reduce or Eliminate Estate Tax** – By setting up a living trust, married persons can double their estate tax exemption from $5.43 million to $10.86 million.

How is a Living Trust Different From a Will?

A living trust is different from a will for two important reasons:

1. Even if you have a will, your estate will still be subject to probate. On the other hand, a living trust will ensure that you will avoid probate.

2. A will is a *public* legal document, which means that the distribution of your estate will be open to the public. On the other hand, a living trust is a *private* document, which means the distribution of your estate will be done in private.

"Funding" the Trust

Setting up a living trust is only the first step in protecting your assets for your designated beneficiaries. But it only works if you "fund" the trust. You must place your assets such as bank accounts, stocks and bonds, mutual funds, and real estate under the name of the trust. This simple but tedious task involves paperwork, and if necessary, the help of an attorney.

Reducing or Eliminating Estate Tax With A/B Trust

By setting up a living trust, married persons can reduce – and possibly – eliminate paying estate tax upon your death by splitting the living trust into 2 separate trusts (A&B) upon the first spouse's death. Splitting the estate into two trusts allows married couples to double the exemption amount; thus, reducing – or even eliminating – estate tax.

Other Necessary Documents of a Typical Living Trust Package

- Advanced Healthcare Directive – An advanced healthcare directive is a legal document that specifies actions that should be taken if you are no longer able to make decisions because of illness or incapacity. This is beneficial because it lessens the stress and on your family to make a difficult decision regarding your end-of-life care should it become necessary.

- Durable Power of Attorney – A durable power of attorney is a legal document that gives someone the authority to act on your financial behalf if you are no longer able to make decisions because of illness or incapacity. Upon your incapacitation, the agent will have the authority to make financial decisions on your behalf.

- Pour-Over Will – The pour-over will is a legal document that works hand-in-hand with the living trust. The pour-over will states that the all the remaining estate at the time of your death will transfer over to the living trust.

- Nomination of Guardian for Minor – The nomination of guardian for minor is a legal document that allows you to appoint a guardian for your minor children after your death. Without this document, the court may appoint a guardian for your children.

- Certification of Trust – The certification of trust is a legal document confirms the trustee's power to act on behalf of the trust. It also provides information on the trust to banks, brokerage firms, and other third parties.

"Building a Legal House"

Setting up a Living Trust (revocable or irrevocable) is relative easy. It's like a lawyer "building" a house – the Trust – for you with a roof and 4 walls. BUT the "house" is empty and would require the owner to "decorate the interior with furniture."

How? Only by funding the Trust with real estate, stocks, mutual funds, checking accounts and life insurance policies could the Owner feel "comfortable" in the house. In another words, a Living Trust Agreement is just a stack of legal paper; and it would be close to worthless if one does NOT fund the trust with those assets listed above.

Conclusion

The living trust is an essential part of every individual's estate planning. By setting up a living trust, you avoid the costly expenses of probate while having the peace of mind that your estate will be distributed according to your desired interests. Furthermore, the living trust also helps reduce and may even eliminate estate tax.

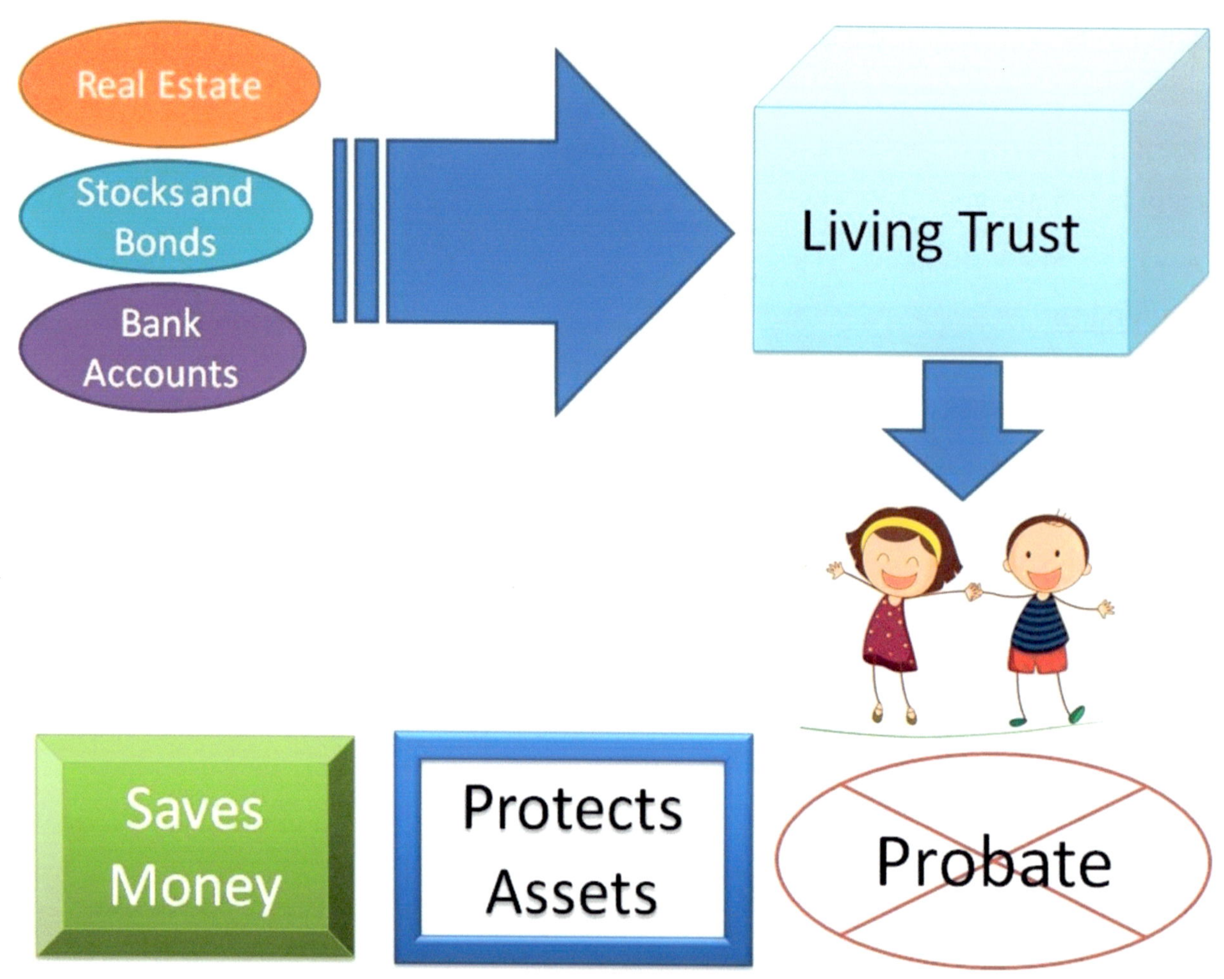
Real Estate
Stocks and Bonds
Bank Accounts
Living Trust
Saves Money
Protects Assets
Probate

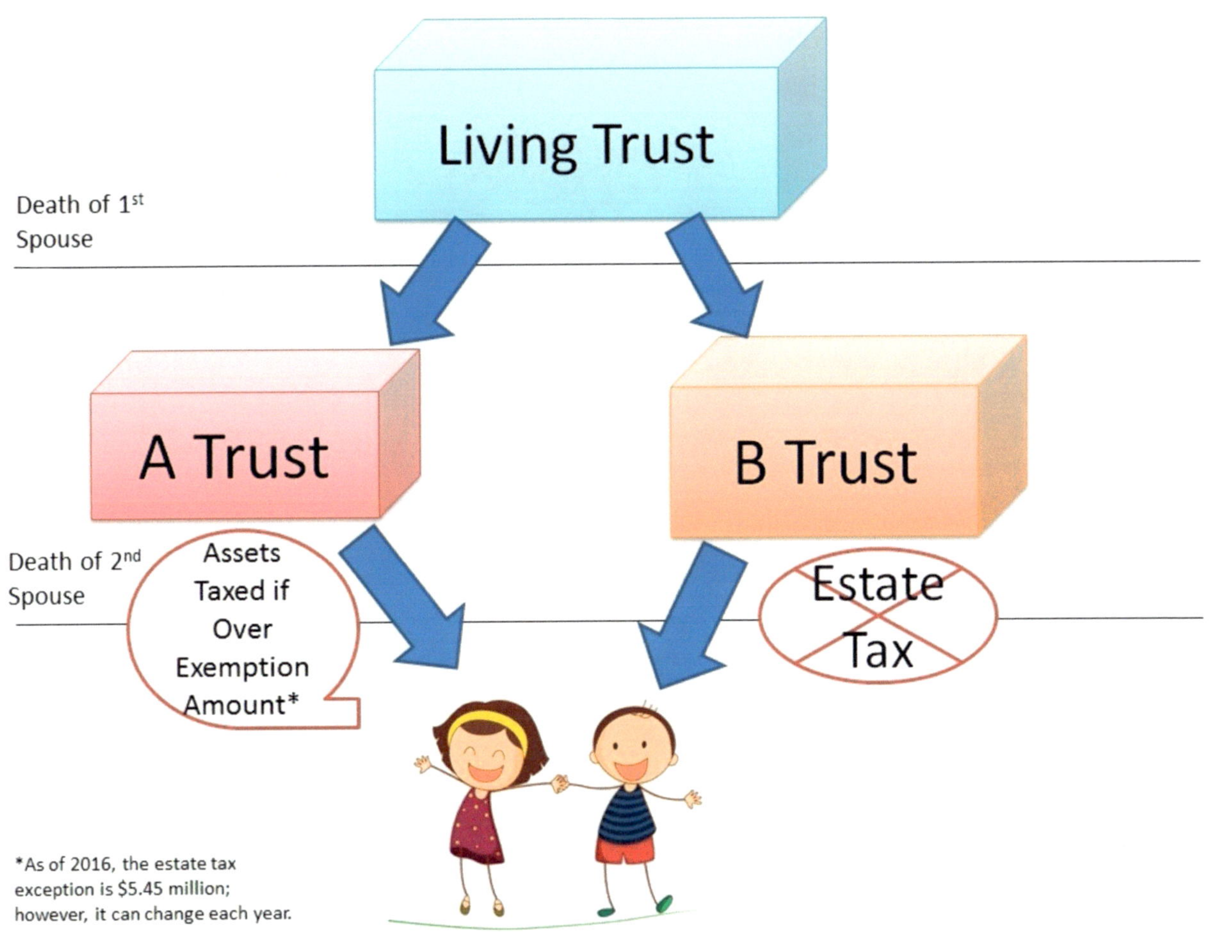

Past 10 Years of Estate Tax Exemption

Year	Exemption Amount	Tax Rate
2007	$2,000,000	45%
2008	$2,000,000	45%
2009	$3,500,000	45%
2010	N/A	0%*
2011	$5,000,000	35%
2012	$5,120,000	35%
2013	$5,250,000	40%
2014	$5,340,000	40%
2015	$5,430,000	40%
2016	$5,450,000	40%

What is Trust?

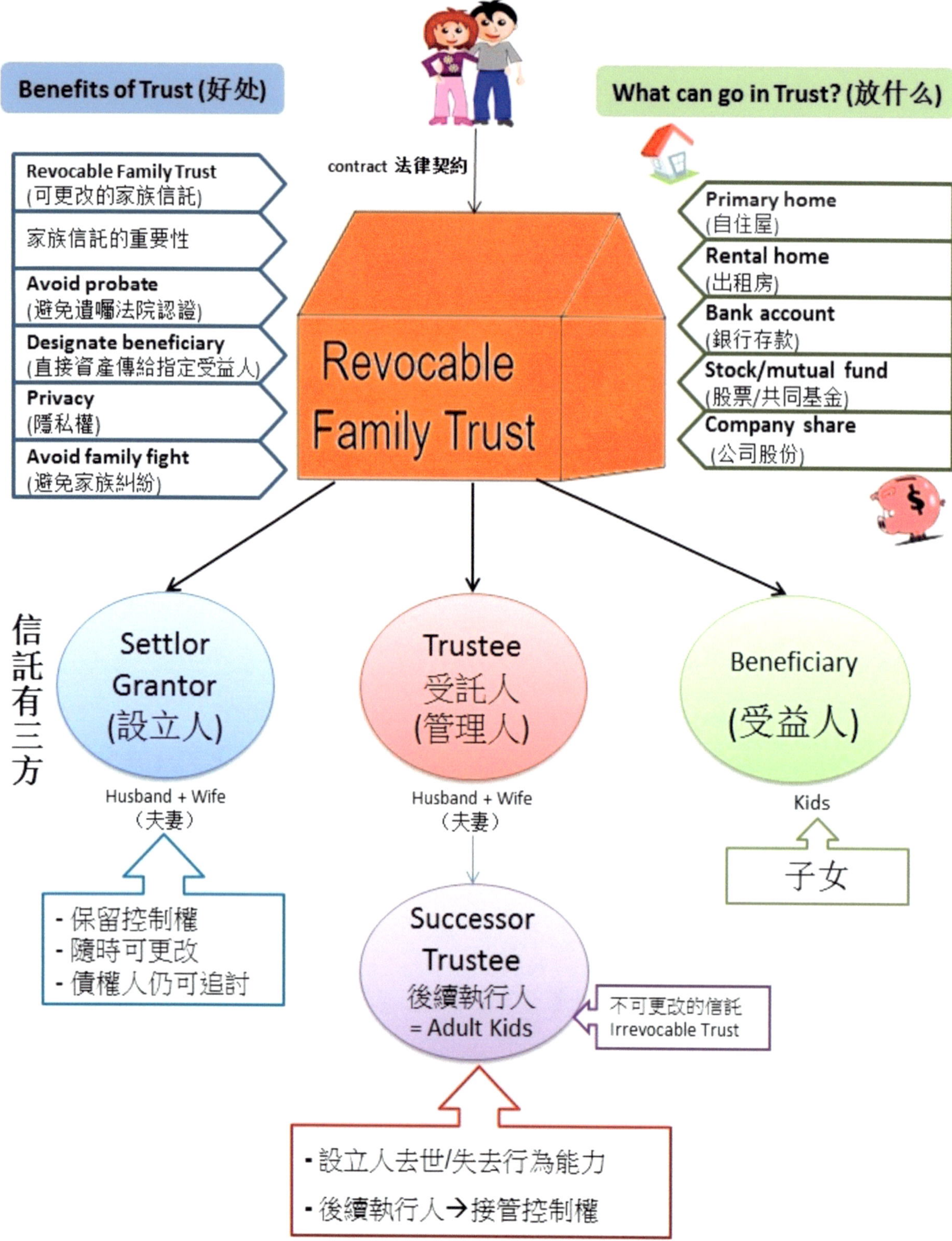

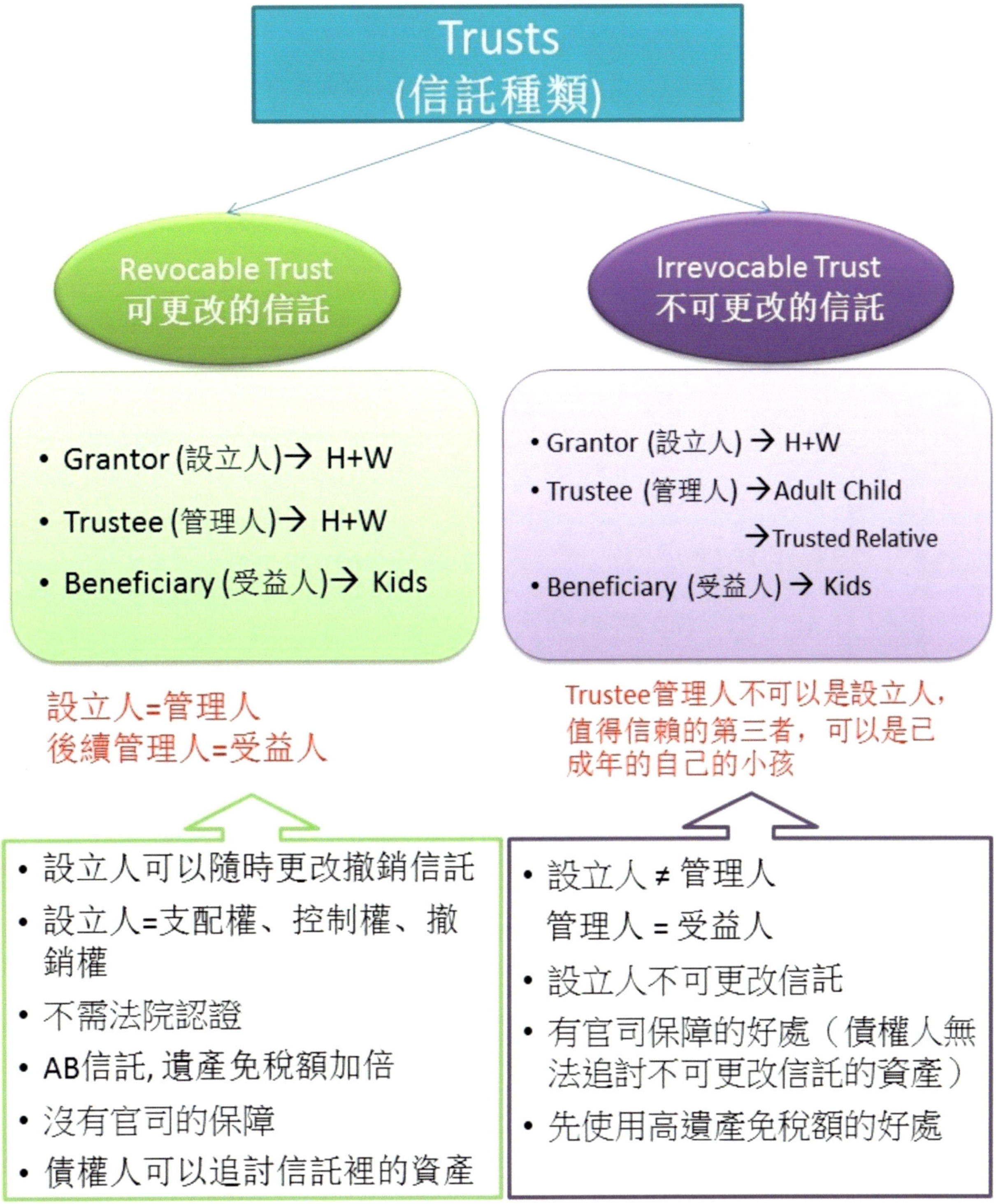

Trusts
(信託種類)

Revocable Trust 可更改的信託

- Grantor (設立人)→ H+W
- Trustee (管理人)→ H+W
- Beneficiary (受益人)→ Kids

設立人=管理人
後續管理人=受益人

- 設立人可以隨時更改撤銷信託
- 設立人=支配權、控制權、撤銷權
- 不需法院認證
- AB信託, 遺產免稅額加倍
- 沒有官司的保障
- 債權人可以追討信託裡的資產

Irrevocable Trust 不可更改的信託

- Grantor (設立人) → H+W
- Trustee (管理人) →Adult Child
  →Trusted Relative
- Beneficiary (受益人) → Kids

Trustee管理人不可以是設立人，值得信賴的第三者，可以是已成年的自己的小孩

- 設立人 ≠ 管理人
  管理人 = 受益人
- 設立人不可更改信託
- 有官司保障的好處（債權人無法追討不可更改信託的資產）
- 先使用高遺產免稅額的好處

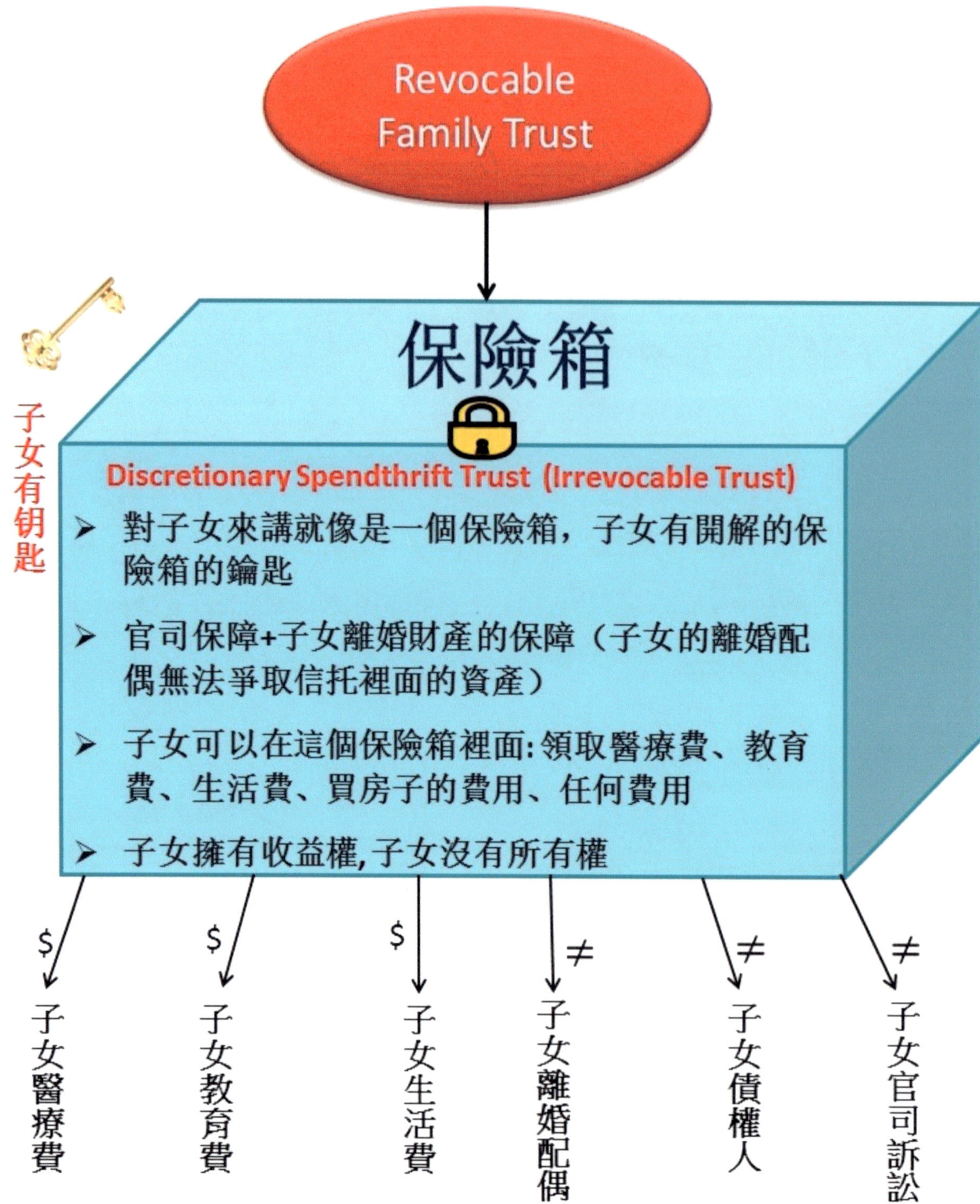
Revocable Family Trust
保險箱
子女有钥匙
Discretionary Spendthrift Trust (Irrevocable Trust)
➢ 對子女來講就像是一個保險箱，子女有開解的保險箱的鑰匙
➢ 官司保障+子女離婚財產的保障（子女的離婚配偶無法爭取信托裡面的資產）
➢ 子女可以在這個保險箱裡面:領取醫療費、教育費、生活費、買房子的費用、任何費用
➢ 子女擁有收益權,子女沒有所有權
$
$
$
≠
≠
≠
子女醫療費
子女教育費
子女生活費
子女離婚配偶
子女債權人
子女官司訴訟

CHAPTER THREE: Irrevocable Trusts

To fully take advantage of the tax benefits offers by IRC Section 7702, many people who have "cash value" life insurance will establish "Irrevocable Life Insurance Trust" (ILIT), to guarantee that their next generation could receive proceeds from a life insurance policy completely TAX-FREE (income tax, capital gains tax and estate tax).

Irrevocable Life Insurance Trust (ILIT)

An ILIT is an irrevocable trust whereby an owner transfers ownership of such policy into an irrevocable Trust.

What are the benefits of an ILIT?

The ILIT is a powerful tool for estate planning purposes. There are three main reasons why an ILIT is useful for protecting your estate:

1. The death benefits from the life insurance policy in the ILIT are not considered part of the grantor's estate. Thus, the life insurance policy will not be subject to estate tax.
2. As a life insurance policy, the death benefits will also not be subject to income tax.
3. Since the assets in the trust are not owned by the grantor or the beneficiaries, they are not subject to creditors.

How does ILIT work?

In a typical life insurance policy, beneficiaries receive benefits ***free of income tax*** upon the death of the policyholders. However, life insurance policies are still considered part of the gross estate of the decedent and subject to ***estate tax.***

By setting up an ILIT, you rescind the ownership of your life insurance by ***transferring*** the life insurance policy into an irrevocable trust. The irrevocable trust becomes the "owner" of the life insurance policy. Because you are no longer the owner of the policy, the life insurance policy is not part of your estate and not subject to estate tax.

By setting up an ILIT, the trust beneficiaries can receive death benefits from the life insurance policy free of ***income tax and estate tax.***

Considerations

In order for the ILIT to work for estate planning, the policyholder must transfer ownership of the life insurance trust three years before her death. If the life insurance policy is transferred within three years of death, the death benefits will still be subject to estate tax.

Irrevocable Trusts

The ILIT is only one example of the power of the irrevocable trust. You do not have to necessarily fund the irrevocable trust with a life insurance policy. You can actually fund the trust with other assets such as bank accounts, stocks, and bonds – while receiving the same tax benefits. This is why the irrevocable trust is such a powerful tool in estate planning.

Conclusion

The ILIT is a useful estate planning tool for individuals with large estates and high assets. Typically, it is used so that the decedent can use the death benefits to pay off estate taxes. It can also be used to insure that the death benefits are received by beneficiaries free of income and estate taxes.

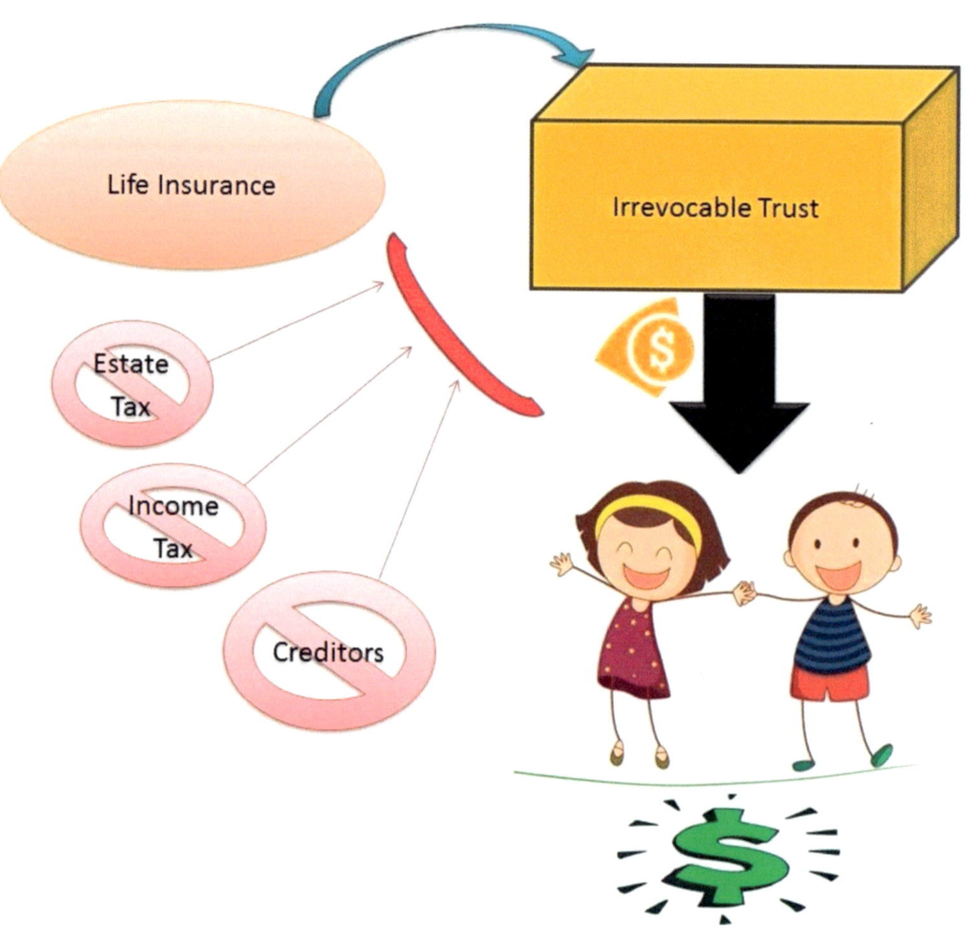
Life Insurance
Irrevocable Trust
Estate Tax
Income Tax
Creditors

Irrevocable Life Insurance Trust
(ILIT)

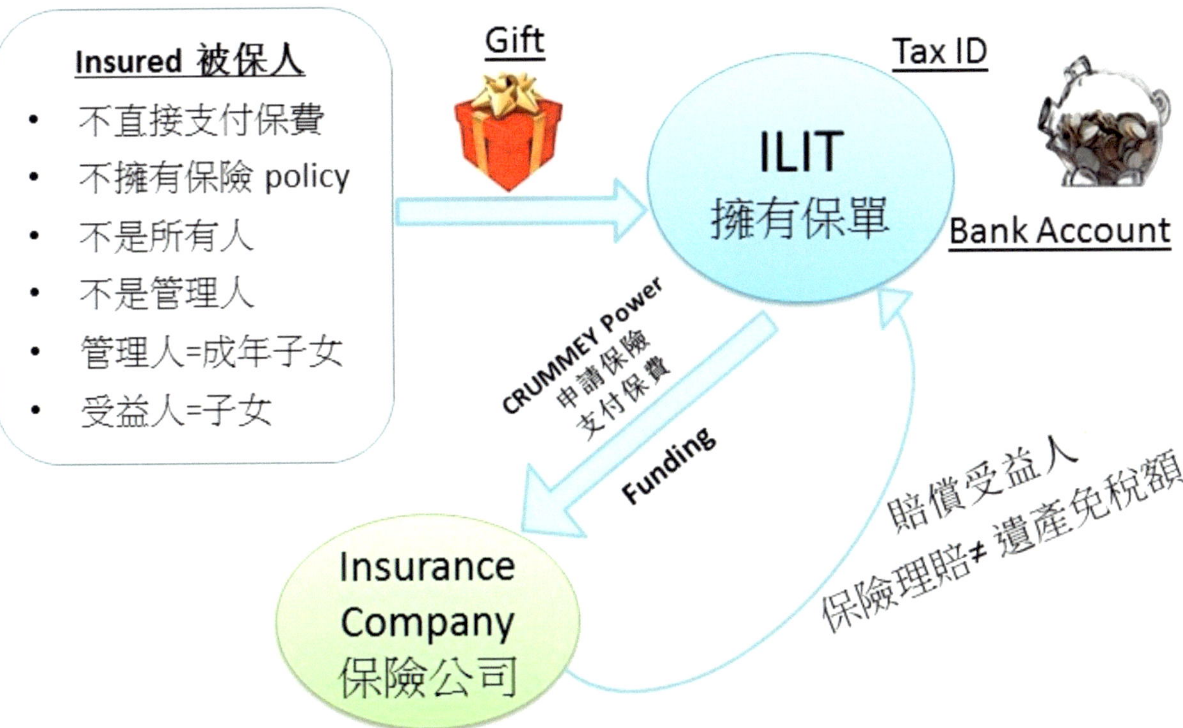

ILIT 擁有保單

被保人透過ILIT, 支付保險公司保費, 當被保人百年歸老的時候，保險公司支付人壽保險理賠金額給受益人，保險理賠的金額，不算是遺產免稅額。

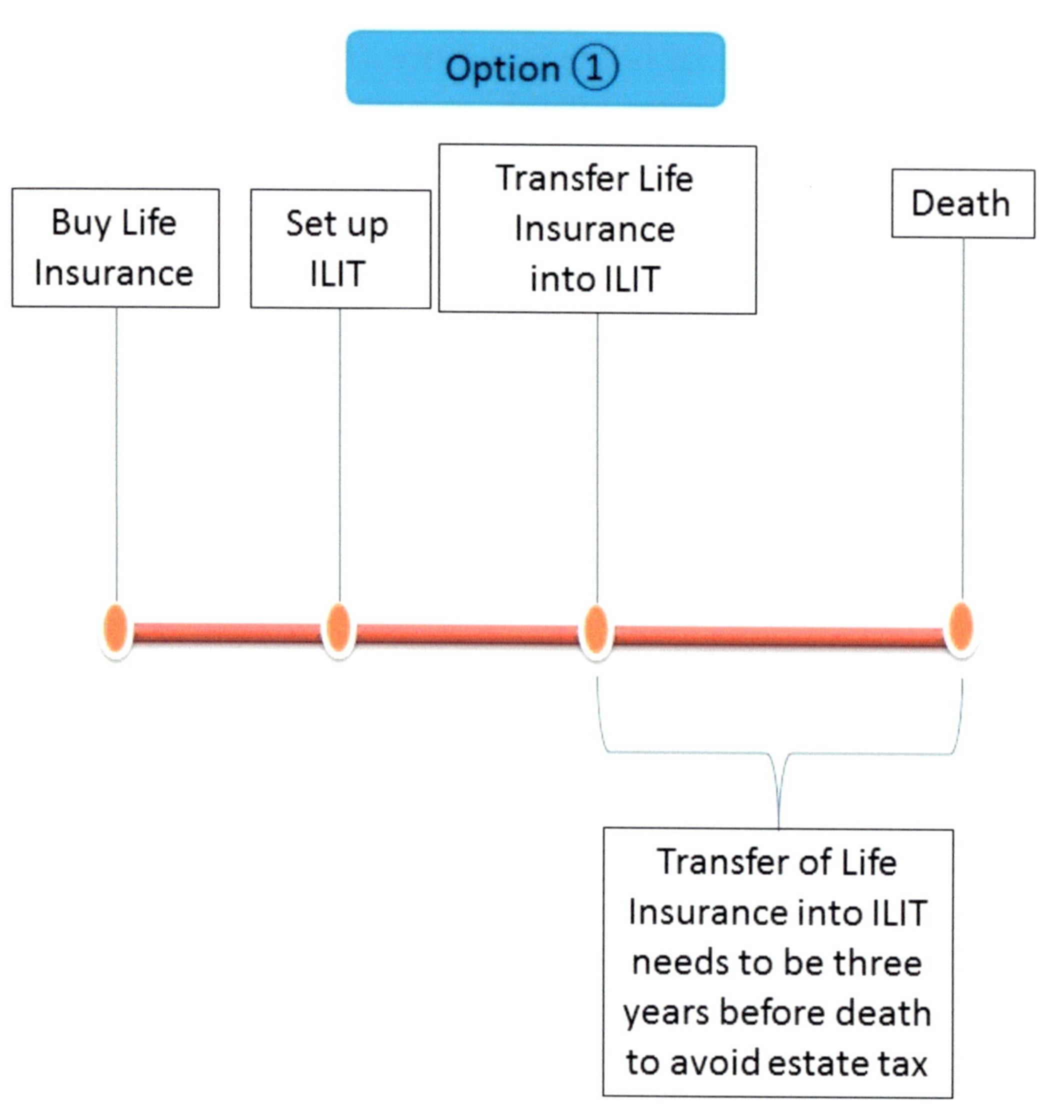
Option ①
Buy Life Insurance
Set up ILIT
Transfer Life Insurance into ILIT
Death
Transfer of Life Insurance into ILIT needs to be three years before death to avoid estate tax

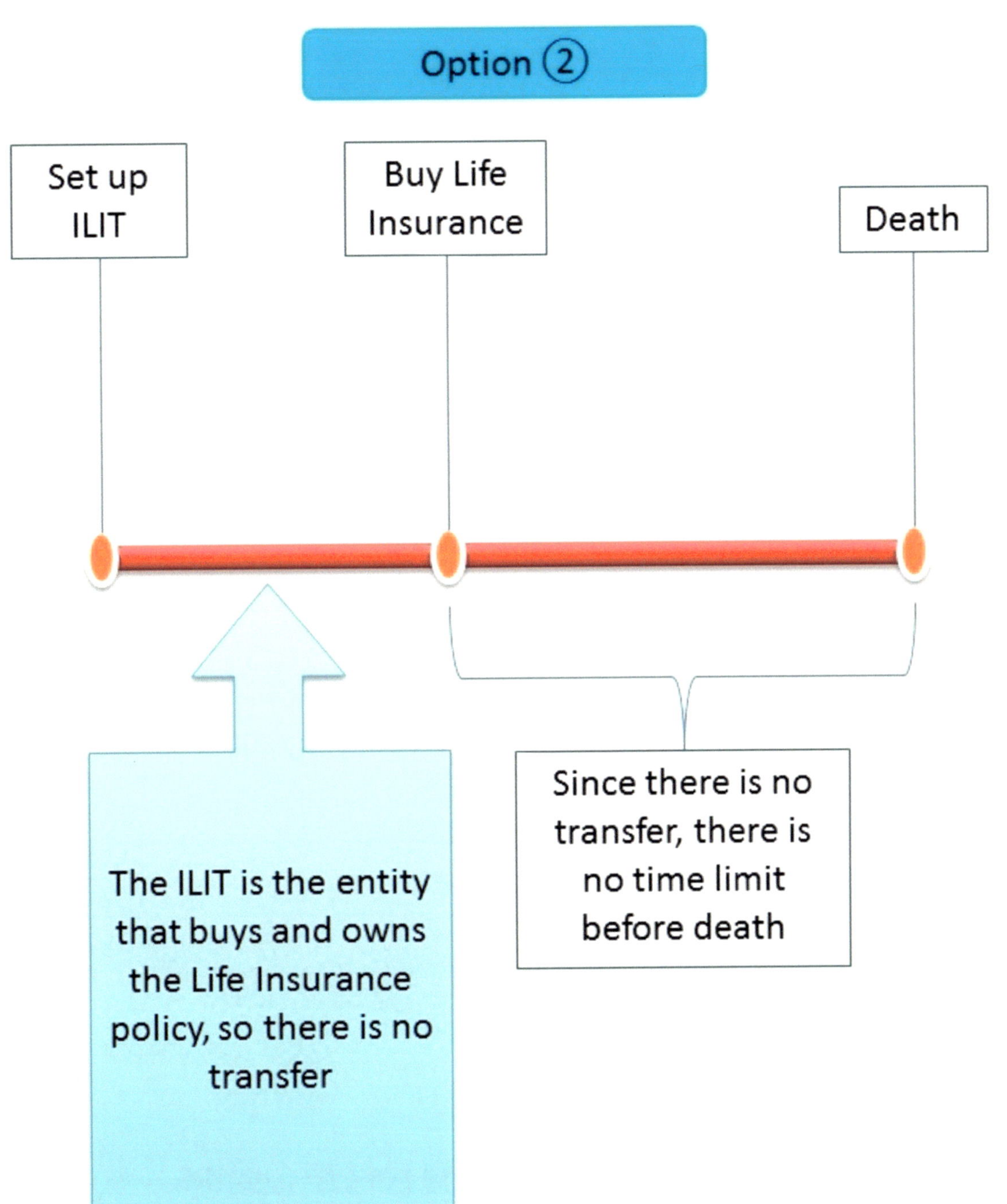
Option ②
Set up ILIT
Buy Life Insurance
Death
The ILIT is the entity that buys and owns the Life Insurance policy, so there is no transfer
Since there is no transfer, there is no time limit before death

ILIT 例子

➢ 按照**2011**的遺產免稅額計算做了**AB**信托，有**$2,000,000**遺產免稅額

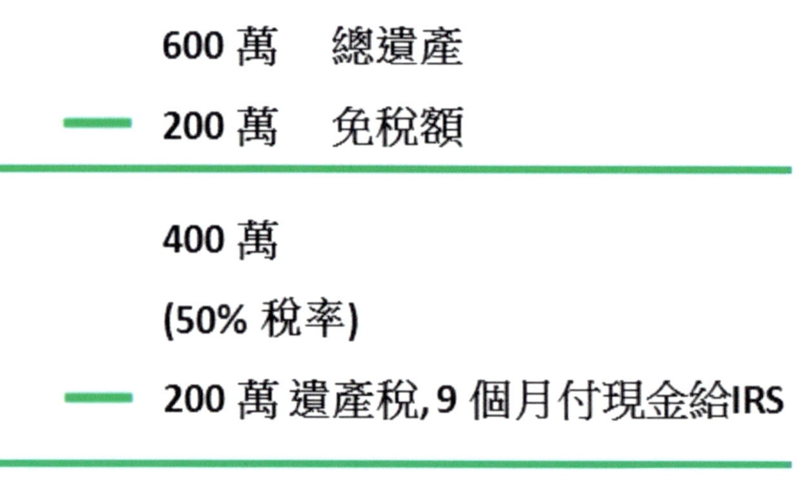

200 萬

高淨值家庭如何做到零遺產稅

- 夫妻 = 1,400 萬的資產
- 2016年百年歸老，現行免稅額度每人545萬
- 設立AB信託 = 免稅額是1,000萬（簡化值）

財產信託化

①避免認證

②遺產免稅額加倍

1,400萬　總資產

— 1,000萬　免稅額

400 萬　遺產打稅的總額

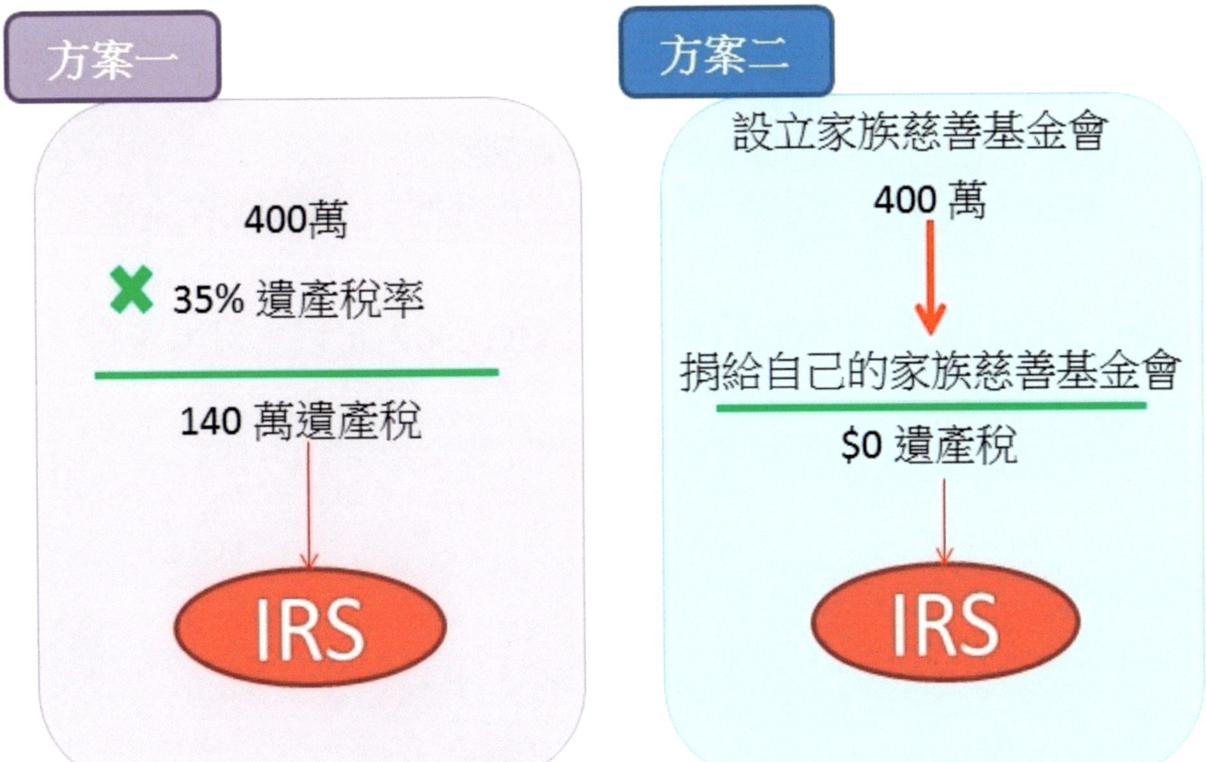

方案一

400萬

✖ 35% 遺產稅率

140 萬遺產稅

IRS

方案二

設立家族慈善基金會

400 萬

捐給自己的家族慈善基金會

$0 遺產稅

IRS

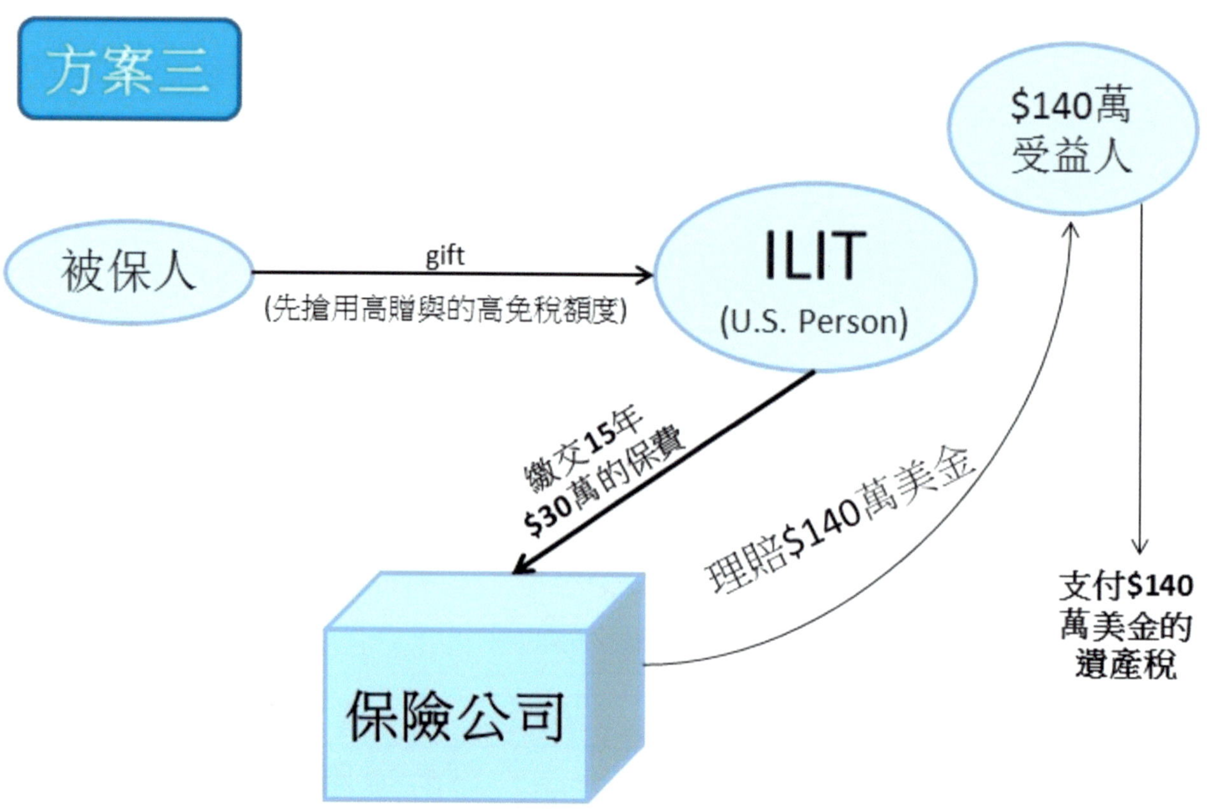

- 被保人 → gift (先搶用高贈與的高免稅額度) → ILIT

  ILIT → 繳交15年總額$300,000的保費
  被保人百年歸老的時候，保險公司理賠$1,400,000美金的金額給受益人（子女）

- 受益人子女，拿著理賠金額$1,400,000，可以支付遺產稅給美國政府。

方案四

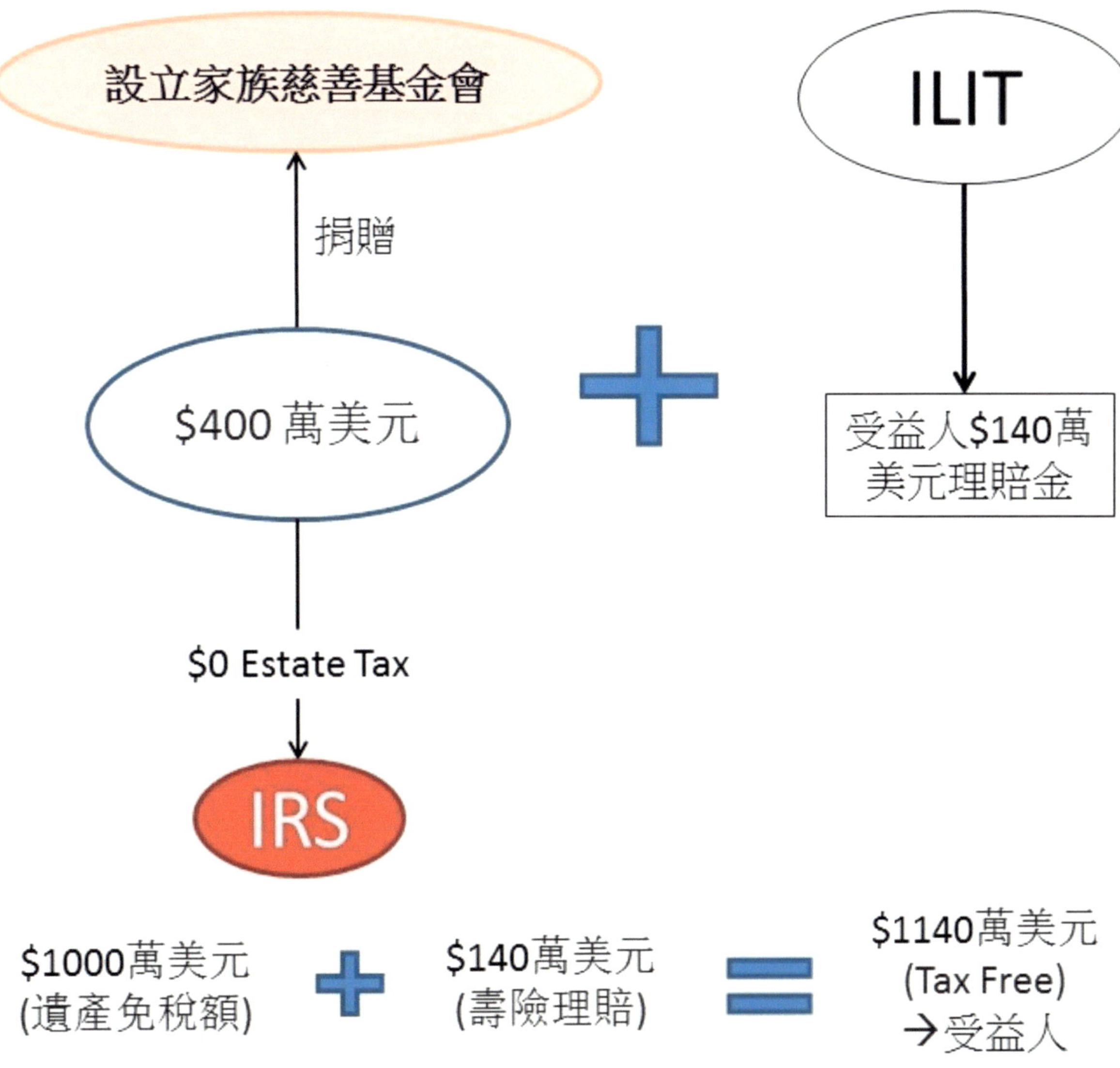

- 設立家族慈善基金會
- 把超過遺產免稅額度的$4,000,000美元捐贈給自己的家族基金會，就不需要繳一毛錢給美國政府國稅局遺產稅。
- ILIT → 受益人又可以領取$1,400,000美元的理賠金額

子女家庭基金會的管理人

支領薪水，繼續做善事

子女領薪水
父母傳承
家族的傳承

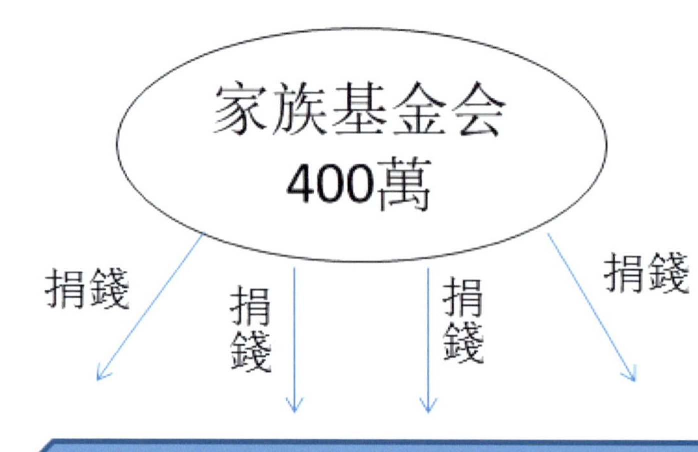

CHAPTER FOUR: Dynasty Trusts

"Dynasty" Trust appears to be all the rage these days, as many lawyers and books tout them. So let's take a look what exactly are "Dynasty" Trust."

Dynasty Trust

The Dynasty Trust is an irrevocable trust created to pass wealth from generation to generation without incurring estate and gift taxes.

In simpler terms, the dynasty trust is the "**ultimate asset protection tool"** to ensure wealth generation for multiple generations – just like a dynasty. Imagine being able to pass your wealth down not only to your children, but to your grandchildren, great-grandchildren, and beyond!

How Do Dynasty Trusts Work?

Dynasty Trusts are like corporations that run in your family to preserve, accumulate, and pass down wealth for generations.
Through a Dynasty Trust, you will be able to:

- Avoid incurring estate taxes
- Avoid incurring gift taxes
- Avoid generation-skipping transfer taxes

How to Create Dynasty Trust

A Dynasty Trust is an ***irrevocable trust*** designed so that it can last forever. Just like an irrevocable trust, you must fund the trust. Examples of assets that can be used to fund a Dynasty Trust include:

- Stocks and bonds
- Bank accounts
- Companies
- Real Estates
- Life Insurance

By placing your assets in a Dynasty Trust, you are no longer legally considered "owner" of these assets, so the assets in this trust are not subject to estate taxes, gift taxes, or generational-skipping taxes.

Benefits for Beneficiaries

After you pass away, your beneficiaries can receive the assets in the trust according to your wishes. Because they don't "own" the assets, they receive the assets without interference from creditors or taxes.

The assets in this trust will continue to pass from generation to generation, according to your stated wishes in the Dynasty Trust.

Is it Possible to Create a Dynasty trust in ALL 50 U.S. States?

NO! As of now, it's NOT possible to create a Dynasty Trust in California, due to the arcane **Rule Against Perpetuities (RAP)**, dating back to times of English Common Law. Basically, RAP states that a Trust – revocable or irrevocable – must terminate during a definite set time limit.

What is Rule Against Perpetuities?

Dynasty Trusts can exist only in states that do not have a Rule Against Perpetuities.

The Rule Against Perpetuities prohibits trusts from existing indefinitely. States such as Colorado, Delaware, Nevada, Virginia, and many others do not have Rules Against Perpetuities. In these states, creating a Dynasty Trust is possible.
In California, RAP exists. The longest period of time a trust can exist is 21 years after the death of last beneficiary. Thus, Dynasty Trusts cannot exist in California.

How About Other States?

Yes! And the good news is that for some states, you <u>don't even need to live there</u> or have any other ties to set up a Dynasty Trust. For example, in the neighboring <u>state of Nevada</u>, it's possible to establish a Dynasty Trust, which maximum time length is <u>365 years</u> – ***longer than the Ming or Ching dynasties!***

Conclusion

Dynasty Trust are clearly complex and would require a team of professionals – lawyers, CPA's financial advisors or planners, stock brokers, real estate and insurance licensees – to structure a trust to suit a family's needs for generation after generation.

CHAPTER FIVE: New Immigrants

New or recent immigrants, especially those who have conditional "green cards, are well-advised to learn the basic concepts of U.S. tax laws because filing tax returns correctly is a pre-condition for becoming a permanent U.S. resident and then a citizen later. Thus, tax compliance is a requirement to "removing conditions" of one's temporary green card or application to become an U.S. citizen.

The good news is that new immigrants can take advantages of tax strategies in this Book the very moment they step on U.S. soil. Again, we like to remind everyone that the law is for everyone, from native born, to "old and new" immigrants alike. If one does not take advantage of laws that are design to apply to everyone, then they've become "second-class" citizens. Of course, we do NOT suggest anyone to become a "second-class" citizen. Thus, for new immigrants, please look the strategies in this book as well.

So How Can New Immigrants Benefit from knowing relevant Tax law?

The best way to answer this question is to present an example.

Example: Dr. X is a foreign national (she is not a U.S. citizen or permanent resident). But she is a very famous surgeon in her native country and comes to America often for conferences and visits. Believing that real estate in America, especially those in the world famous *Newport Coast* area, are a good investment, Dr. X paid ***$5 million in cash*** for an ocean view mansion in a gated community in 2015.

It's now 2016 and now Dr. X. needs to raise cash for another business venture in her home country. She sells the Newport Coast home for $5 million, and believes that she doesn't have to pay any tax because there is no gain. <u>Is she correct?</u>

NO!! Under CA tax law, there is a 3.33% withholding tax – of the total sales price – is the Seller is a foreigner. So the Escrow Company will **withhold $116,667** from Dr. X.

Thus, by reading this Book, New and "Old" immigrants, old and young, whether you are native or not, the concepts illustrated here could help those in need. **Can New Immigrants Take Advantage of the "4 Law Sections that everyone must know," perhaps even before they arrive in America?**

<u>Yes!</u> Especially for Section 121 (Primary Home Capital gains exemption).

For example, Mr. and Mrs. Chen arrived in America on an EB-5 (investor) visa that turned into a *conditional* green card. After 2 years here, they "removed conditions" on the green card and became permanent residents. Since they gained permanent residency, they decided to sell their Shanghai house, which they lived for many years before coming to America (purchase price $500K, sales price $1 Million). So Mr. and Mrs. Chen **claim Section 121 capital gains exemption** for a house in China, which they lived <u>before even coming to America</u>?

The answer is Yes! Due to the fact that U.S. tax law takes into consideration "worldwide income and assets." And since Section 121 allows for capital gain exemption for married couples if they lived in their primary home "2 of past 5 years," then the sale of the Chen residence in Shanghai also qualifies for the exemption. Again, Section does NOT require the owners to be living in the subject property at time of sale.

Thus, new immigrants like the Chen family can enjoy tax benefits for assets acquired before gaining U.S. residency or even stepping foot on American soil.

Conclusion

Many recent immigrants came to U.S. with the EB-5 visa, their first taste of benefits under U.S. laws. To help them further integrate into American society, we suggest new immigrants learning more about tax laws, especially those outlined in this Book. If you are a "New Immigrant," you may as well learn the benefits of tax law and take full advantage of them.

Frequently Asked Questions (FAQ)

Frequently Asked Questions (FAQ) for Asset Protection And Tax Minimization

What is the first thing one should do if s/he wants to learn more about Asset Protection and Tax Minimization?

One should gain as much knowledge as possible in this area. While there are many books (in bookstore or in Amazon) on areas of Personal Finance, we have yet to find a book devoted exclusive to this important subject. That is one of the primary reasons we are writing this Book, to provide consumers and others who are interested in this subject a place to find valuable information.

What Does the Time Value of Money Have to Do Anything With Tax Law or Asset Protection?

Time Value of Money

Another concept that is indispensable to asset protection is "Time Value of Money." Basically, if one can save money – ***year after year*** – from paying taxes, the money saved can grow into something big, **Real Big**. How big?

Here is a simplistic view of on the future value of money. Assume you can save $10,000 in taxes each year, and you do so for the next 40 years, how much will you have? (Assuming the rate of inflation = 3%)

Most people will be tempted to say around $400,000 (40 years x $10,000). And with such a low inflation rate, it *couldn't* be much more than $400,000, right?

They would actually be way OFF target, as the answer is **$754,000!!** Why? That's the magic of compounded growth, WITHOUT taxes taking a bite. So if you can save $10,000 annually in taxes that would turn into $754,000 in 40 years (or $475,000 over 30 years). THAT is “Asset Protection.”

Is there a way to “take care” of all tax problems at once while offering the best asset protection?

There is no panacea *per se*. However, we believe knowledge is power and indeed could be a panacea to solve the problem of savings tax efficiently, which translates into asset protection.

Why is anything to do with Life Insurance have a negative connotation?

A strong Asset Protection plan must involve a plan to reduce taxes, and one of the best way to minimize taxes (federal and state) is under the “umbrella” of IRC section 7702 – the section on Life Insurance.

A quick search on Internet would reveal that, somehow, the term “life insurance’ has some sort of a negative connation. Furthermore, if one bring up the term ‘life insurance” with friends and family members, the usual response is a concerned look and perhaps even doubt. Some friends and family members might even chime in with their “not so good” experiences.”

Thus, we suggest you ask a simple question – what is the difference between IRC Section 7702 v. Life Insurance? Answer: there is not a difference, as they refer to the exact SAME thing!

Why does IRC Section 7702 appears more formal and what can consumer learn from it?

Perhaps the fact it refers to a specific code section of the law, Section 7702 appears very formal in appearance. Thus, if anyone have doubts about this section of the law, they should conduct their own research into this subject, or consult an expert (lawyer or tax CPA). AND they should cast doubts on this section of the law before trying to understand it.

It's our duties as lawyers to inform the public and consumers that beneficial parts of certain laws. From an Asset protection and Tax Minimization point of view, it would be hard for any lawyer of tax CPA to disagree with the fact that Section 7702 (Life Insurance) is an excellent vehicle to save taxes and protect one's assets.

Thus, consumers could advise their friends and/or family members who are not familiar with Section 7702 that they should study this subject more before just merely following hearsay on the Internet.

There are lots of information out in the Internet and in the market place. There are also lots of financial "scams" out there. What should ordinary consumers do to avoid being such scams?

The first thing a consumer must check is whether the speaker who hold represents himself/herself as "an expert" in Asset protection and Tax Minimization or related fields holds any type of professional license (attorney, CPA, Insurance, etc.). Having a license at least show one has minimum knowledge and training in this area.

However, this area of law is complex; just because one says s/he is an "expert" does not mean that's case. Rather, consumers should take actions to ensure the "expert" is indeed knowledgeable.

What are some factors one could use to see if a "so-called expert" is indeed an expert?

Specifically, consumer should ask questions such as is the expert is part of a professional team, including lawyers, CPA's, real estate brokers/agents, and insurance licensees.

Again, the areas of Asset Protection and Tax Minimization are complex and require multiple professionals to design a customized plan for different clientele. It would difficult for ***anyone person*** to state that s/he is an expert on Asset Protection and Tax Minimization, or on IRC sections 7702 or 1031 without part of a professional team. We have yet to find any one person in Southern California who is equally knowledgeable in the IRC section cited in this book – Sections 121, 1031, 1035 and 7702.

Furthermore, to empower consumers, we suggest asking one question to anyone who is representing himself as an expert (in anything) – "Can you please cite the relevant law to support your position?" This way, consumers could test out any "expert" to see if s/he is knowledgeable or just want to "sell you something."

Why should teenagers understand the value of money and "Asset Protection and Tax Minimization"?

Teenagers and young people have something that's **FAR MORE valuable** than their middle-aged parents – time. By knowing the "laws of compound interest" and the laws stated in this book, they could grow and then preserve a large portfolio of assets, even if they start in small amounts

Why is the knowledge of tax law so indispensable in Asset Protection?

By now, it should be obvious that tax is **a liability** for everyone. If you could decrease the amount of tax you pay, then obviously you've engaged in Asset Protection. The MORE you save, the MORE of your assets **you protect**.

It appears that integral part of an Asset Protection Plan would involve life insurance and/or annuities. But I've heard that many companies that sell life insurance and annuities operate like "Pyramid Schemes." What can I do to protect myself?

First, the term "pyramid" probably describes ***every*** company's structure in America. Isn't there only one CEO at the very top, and then more middle managers, and then a large number of employees at the ***bottom***?

The above structure looks like a pyramid no matter how one looks at it. Specifically, famous companies such as Google, Amazon, Apple, Citibank, New York Life, etc. ***all*** have this structure.

Perhaps consumer heard that supervisors and/or managers receive an "override" based on sales of those "below them" – which ostensibly give an even more appearance of "pyramid." BUT for those who understand how U.S. corporations work, what company does NOT reward their executives with an increase in sales or a percentage of sale?

Even in law firms, which also have a pyramid management structure, profit sharing is based mostly on those partners who are "rainmakers" – those who bring in most fees.

Further, it's very common in the finance industry to spread out compensation amongst supervisors and those below them. Thus, with a "pyramid" corporate structure and a compensation system that have overrides, financial and life insurance companies are just like any other company in America,

Thus, it's our opinion that just because a company have a pyramid corporate structure and compensation system that have overrides, that fact alone shouldn't disqualify a company from your list of product providers. Rather, one should engage in "due diligence" with an open mind, perhaps even comparing different companies. Indeed, learning more about different financial companies that serves ***your needs*** would just increase your knowledge – since knowledge is power.

Conclusion

Congratulations! You have now worked through the entire book! We are sure that you are now a *more knowledgeable* than when you first started.

By completing this book, you should have learned:

- 4 Basic Tax Laws That Will Save You ***BIG*** on Taxes!
- How to Structure a Real Estate Transaction Without Ever Paying Capital Gains Tax (You and Your Heirs)
- How to Change Primary Homes Every 2-5 Years – TAX FREE
- How to "***Step Up***" Your Basis in Real Estate Such That Your Heirs Can Inherit TAX FREE
- How to "Exchange" Your Investments (Real Estate and Investment) Into Like-Kind Investment to **Defer Your Taxes**

AND …

- Carry a TOOLBOX to Pass Your Hard-Earned Assets to the Next Generation, and a MAP to create Your Legacy!

Is Avoiding Taxes Illegal?

If avoiding taxes is illegal, then the ultra-rich, or anyone with knowledge of tax law, is "guilty." Let's ask ourselves another question: does possessing knowledge of the law itself means one is "guilty" of "tax avoidance"? That wouldn't make too much sense since possessing knowledge of the law ***in America****, a country ruled by the Law,* should be encouraged.

Unfortunately, the tax code is so complex that many ordinary citizens find themselves practically "going in circles" while trying to understand even the basic provisions of the Internal Revenue Code (IRC).

That's why we've painstakingly analyze different sections of the IRC, and then "distilled" such knowledge in this book. Most specifically, we searched for provisions that BENEFIT "Personal Finance" – and NOT those of companies – to **level the playing field** for ordinary people, new immigrants, or anyone who wishes to learn more about "Personal Finance Tax Lax" to protect themselves.

Integrate into America

At a time in America where the divide between the "rich" and the "poor" is widening, where many new immigrants find it hard to assimilate into America because all the complex laws, this Book will provide a Road Map to help those new immigrants integrate into American society. Understanding the laws of America is the first step become a productive citizen of this country.

Furthermore, whether you are a new immigrant, or a native son or daughter of this country, our book will allow you to "Level the Playing Field" with the knowledge in this book. No longer would you wonder why your take-home pay is ***only about half*** of your "gross salary" if you are single (due to various types of taxes) and am a salaried employee. No longer would you wonder how Warren Buffett, one of the world's richest, would have a ***lower tax rate*** than his secretary.

We have seen or heard "complaints" that new immigrants sometimes don't integrate into American culture by not learning to speak English. Well, we have a novel way to "force" new immigrants to learn English ***faster***. If new immigrants knows American laws that would benefit them and protect them, which would be a great incentive to learn those laws. Thus, by learning U.S. laws, that would force the same immigrants to have more of an urgency to learn English. In effect, learning the law would allow immigrants to assimilate more easily into the American culture.

Overview of Saving Taxes and Asset Protection

This book is meant to provide an overview of tax laws that allows one to save on their taxes easily. The U.S. tax laws are complex and convoluted. As tax experts, we've taken years to understand the most important parts and then present those parts in an "easy to understand" manner in this book. We can confidently say that there is no other book like this in the marketplace, as this book provides materials and concepts filtered by our vast experience in this area.

First, we will introduce basic, easy-to-follow concepts and illustration that anyone can understand ***instantly.*** We are confident that everyone would be able to apply one or more of our "4 Basic Tax Laws to Tax-Never" ***immediately*** or in the foreseeable future. Applying all 4 of these laws will provide solid foundation for you **NOT** to pay taxes for life. EVEN BETTER – applying one of more of these laws, plus some estate planning, and your heirs would NOT have to any Estate Tax!

Our basic premise is knowledge sharing, especially on areas of personal finance and tax laws, subjects that not taught in college or **even in Law School!**

Once again, it is our intent to ***provide everyone – from the young to the old*** – easy to understand concepts to pay as little tax as possible, so you could have MORE money for your FAMILY!

For now, we wish you the best of luck! Knowledge is POWER!

Made in the USA
Columbia, SC
22 February 2024